Solo Parenting:

Your Essential Guide to Navigating the Pains, Challenges, and Triumphs

By Jennifer Gill

Solo Parenting:

Your Essential Guide to Navigating the Pains, Challenges, And Triumphs

Written By Jennifer Gill

Created With Support From

Illustration Team Fay Michelle

Jacqueline Nero-Douglas / Carl M. Douglas
ComfortLegacies@gmail.com

Solo Parenting:

Your Essential Guide to Navigating the Pains, Challenges, And Triumphs

Written by Jennifer Gill

©2024 Jennifer Gill

All rights reserved. No part of this publication may be reproduced, distributed, or transmitted in any form or by any means, including photocopying, recording, or other electronic or mechanical methods, without the prior written permission of the publisher, except in the case of brief quotations embodied in critical reviews and certain other noncommercial uses permitted by copyright law.

Printed in the USA.

Written by Jennifer Gill

Created with Support from Team Fay Michelle

Jacqueline Nero-Douglas / Carl M. Douglas

Dedication

To my beautiful daughters, whose unwavering love and boundless spirit have been my greatest source of strength. May you always know that love, resilience, and the unbreakable bond between us are the true pillars of our lives. Thank you for being my inspiration and my heart's greatest joy. This guide is also for every solo mother who faces the world with courage and determination, and for the incredible journey we share.

Table of Contents

Dedication 4

Introduction 14

Chapter 1: Solo Parenting 23

An Overview: Understanding Solo Parenting 25

What Is Solo Parenting? 25

The Challenges of Solo Parenting 26

The Triumphs of Solo Parenting 26

Chapter 2: Stigmas 29

Societal Stereotypes 29

Misconceptions about Single-Parent Families 30

The Impact of Stigma 30

Breaking the Stigma 31

Chapter 3: Emotional Struggles 33

Grief and Loss 33

Isolation and Loneliness 34

Anxiety and Worry 35

Guilt and Self-Blame...........36

Chapter 4: Feeling Overwhelmed as a Single Parent 38

Recognize the Signs of Overwhelm...........38
Prioritize Self-Care...........39
Seek Support...........39
Create a Routine...........40
Practice Mindfulness...........40
Break Tasks Down into Smaller Steps...........40
Practice Gratitude...........40

Chapter 5: Dealing with Loneliness as a Single Parent 42

Acknowledge Your Feelings...........42
Build a Support System...........43
Schedule Social Activities...........43
Practice Self-Care...........43
Seek Professional Help...........44

Chapter 6 Financial Challenges 45

Understanding Your Income and Expenses...........46
Reducing Expenses...........46
Increasing Your Income...........47

Saving for the Future 47

Seeking Support 48

Chapter 7: Managing a Single-Income Household 49

Create a Realistic Budget 49

Prioritize Necessary Expenses 50

Seek Out Assistance 50

Increase Your Income 51

Chapter 8: Savings, Insurance, and Retirement 52

Savings 52

Insurance 53

Retirement 55

Chapter 9: Time Management 57

Create a Schedule 57

Prioritize Tasks 58

Set Realistic Goals 58

Limit Distractions 58

Make Time for Yourself 59

Chapter 10: Balancing Work and Parenting as a Single Parent 61

Establish a Routine 61
Set Boundaries 62
Seek Support 62
Prioritize and Organize 62
Consider Flexible Work Arrangements 63
Embrace Imperfection 63
Create Quality Time 63
Engage in Self-Care and Personal Growth 64
Think about Financial Planning 64
Use Open Communication 64

Chapter 11: Self-Care and Personal Time 66

The Importance of Self-Care 66
Making Time for Self-Care 67
Personal Time 68

Chapter 12: Building Strong Bonds 71

Chapter 13: Nurturing Emotional Connection 75

Be Present and Engaged 75
Show Empathy and Understanding 76

    Spend Quality Time Together 76
    Express Your Love and Affection 77
    Be a Role Model 77

Chapter 14: Quality Time 78
    Schedule It In 78
    Be Present 79
    Ask for Their Input 79
    Keep It Simple 79
    Make It Routine 80
    Be Flexible 80
    Enjoy the Moment 80

Chapter 15: Developing Resilience as a Single Parent
.... 81
    Understanding Resilience 81
    Building Resilience 82
    The Benefits of Resilience 84

Chapter 16: Overcoming Obstacles 85
    Financial Challenges 85
    Emotional Challenges 86
    Social Challenges 87

Parenting Challenges 87

Chapter 17: Embracing Change as a Single Parent .. 89
Change Brings Growth 89
Change Encourages Flexibility 90
Change Fosters Resilience 90
Change Promotes Positive Thinking 91
Change Encourages Self-Care 91

Chapter 18: Celebrate 93
The Power of Celebrating Success 93
Ideas for Celebrating Success 94

Chapter 19: Wins 97

Chapter 20: Goals 100
Step 1: Define Your Goals 100
Step 2: Create a Plan 101
Step 3: Take Action 102
Step 4: Celebrate Your Successes 102

Chapter 21: Support Systems 104
Building a Support Network: A Key to Successful Solo Parenting 104
What Is a Support Network? 105
Why Is Building a Support Network Important? 105
How to Build a Support Network 106

Chapter 22: Family and Friends 110
Sharing the Load 110
Emotional Support 111
Socialization for Your Children 111
How to Build Your Support Network 111

Chapter 23: Connecting with Other Single Parents 114
Benefits of Connecting with Other Single Parents 114
Ways to Connect with Other Single Parents 115

Chapter 24: Government Assistance 119
Canada 119
United States 124

Chapter 25: Government Aid and Grants for Single Parents 127

Types of Government Aid and Grants In The US 127

Applying for Government Aid and Grants 130

Chapter 26: Community Programs 131

Government Assistance Programs 131

Local Community Resources 132

Online Support Communities 133

Scholarships and Educational Resources 133

Chapter 27: Creating a Stable and Nurturing Environment 135

Establish a Routine 135

Create a Consistent Home 136

Provide Emotional Support 136

Foster a Positive Environment 136

Take Care of Yourself 137

Chapter 28: Establishing Routines: A Key to Successful Solo Parenting 138

Chapter 29: Fostering Open Communication 142

Create a Safe Space 142

Listen Actively *143*
Validate Their Feelings *143*
Use Simple and Clear Language *143*
Encourage Honesty *144*
Practice Patience *144*
Lead by Example *144*

Chapter 30: Growing as a Single Parent 145

Growth Mindset *145*
Self-Care *146*
Building a Support Network *147*
Personal Development *147*
Embracing Change *148*

Chapter 31: Resource Books 149

Books *149*

Inspirational Quotes for Single Parents 150

In Conclusion 154

Introduction

Welcome to a journey of resilience, strength, and unwavering love. As a single mother who raised two incredible daughters with little to no support, I understand the challenges, sacrifices, and triumphs that come with this path. This book is a testament to our collective strength and a guide to navigating the unique journey of single parenthood.

Here, you will find practical advice and encouragement. Whether you're just beginning this journey or have been walking this path for some time, know that you are not alone. Together, we can celebrate the victories, share the burdens, and empower one another to raise our children with love, courage, and grace.

Thank you for joining me on this journey. May this book inspire and support you as you continue to build a beautiful and fulfilling life for you and your children.

I am a mother, fiercely devoted to my girls. Our lives, though challenging, are filled with love and determination.

My older daughter faced unique challenges. She was raised in a household where English was seldom spoken. My in-laws, who helped care for my daughters as I worked long hours to make ends meet, spoke only Punjabi. This created a barrier for my oldest daughter, who struggled to grasp English as her primary language. As she entered school, her difficulty with English became apparent, leading to academic setbacks and the need for expensive tutoring sessions that stretched my budget thin.

On the other hand, my younger daughter had a different experience. I tried to give her every advantage that I could, and encouraged her to watch cartoons and educational programs in English. With her young and absorbent mind, she quickly picked up the language. She excelled in school initially, bringing home good grades that filled my heart with pride.

However, as she progressed through school, signs began to appear that she, too, might need extra help, just as my older daughter had. The cost of tutoring for two daughters was overwhelming for me as I worked tirelessly as a driver to support my family.

My husband, disinterested in the lives of his daughters, offered no financial or emotional support. His traditional views and disappointment in not having a son weighed heavily on my heart, but I never let it affect my dedication to my daughters. I was their rock, their provider, and their source of unwavering love.

Despite the challenges, I remained resilient. I sought help from community programs. I found a tutor for my oldest daughter who could relate to her struggles with language barriers and learning disabilities.

As the years passed, my daughter improved in her studies with the help of dedicated tutors. Her teachers did not understand her challenges. With the support of the tutoring she received, she overcame her academic struggles.

Through it all, my love and determination never faltered. I tried very hard to juggle work, parenting, and the emotional toll of being a single mother with grace and strength. My daughters grew up knowing the value of hard work, resilience, and unwavering love.

Today, my daughters and I share an unbreakable bond. Our story is one of triumph over adversity, of love, of overcoming obstacles, and of a fierce determination. I was determined to give my daughters a brighter future, no matter the challenges I faced along the way.

My journey as a single mother was marked by more than just financial and educational challenges. My path was scarred by the emotional wounds left by my husband.

Family members urged me to leave the toxic relationship for good, but I did not.

My siblings and parents provided solace and clarity during these dark times. They reassured me that I was capable of providing a safe and loving home for my daughters on my own. They encouraged me to seek legal counsel and take steps to ensure my and my children's security. Despite their unwavering support, I hesitated. I harbored a deep love for my husband, clinging to the hope that things could somehow work out for the sake of our family.

But hope can only last so long in the face of ongoing neglect and abuse. The deterioration of our relationship became undeniable, leaving me with no choice but to navigate the challenges of single parenthood alone. However, I did not get a divorce. I was still married, but did life on my own without any help from my husband.

It was a time of uncertainty and adjustment, but I was determined to create a safe haven where my daughters could thrive.

The road ahead was not easy. I faced financial hardships, balancing work and child care responsibilities while dealing with the emotional aftermath of leaving an abusive relationship. There were moments of doubt and exhaustion, but I drew strength from the love for my girls.

They became my reason to persevere, to strive for a better life despite the obstacles in my path.

As the girls grew older, they became my pillars of strength as well. They understood the sacrifices that I had made for them and embraced their roles as my cheerleaders and supporters. Together, we faced the world as a team, celebrating each milestone and triumph, no matter how small.

My journey as a single mother is a testament to my unwavering love, resilience, and courage in the face of adversity. I had emerged from the shadows of an abusive relationship stronger and more determined than ever to provide my daughters with a future filled with hope and possibilities. We are a family bound not by blood alone, but by the unbreakable bonds of love and resilience forged through hardship and triumph.

Despite the strides that I made being married without help, new challenges emerged on my journey. As my daughters progressed through school, they encountered prejudices that added to their already difficult circumstances. Their instructors, who often couldn't relate to their experiences as children of a single mother from a minority background, sometimes showed a lack of understanding and empathy.

My oldest daughter, with her learning disability exacerbated by language barriers, faced particularly harsh treatment from some teachers who didn't make accommodations for her needs. She encountered subtle biases that made her feel like an outsider at times.

I am fiercely protective of my daughters, and I noticed these injustices and felt a rising frustration. I considered seeking legal assistance to address the discrimination my daughters faced in school. The lack of support from a spouse made the uphill battle of advocating for my children's rights even more daunting.

Despite these challenges, I refused to let prejudice hold my daughters back. I attended parent-teacher conferences armed with research and legal information, advocating fiercely for both of my daughter's right to receive appropriate educational support and for her to be treated fairly. I sought advice from any and all organizations that supported minority families and single parents, gathering resources and strategies to navigate the complexities of educational inequality.

Some teachers, moved by my persistence and dedication, started to make efforts to understand the learning challenges better and provide the support my daughter needed. My daughter learned to speak up for herself and challenge biased assumptions, earning the respect of her peers and teachers alike.

Through it all, I instilled in my daughters a sense of resilience and self-worth. I like to think that I taught them to stand up for what was right and to never let anyone diminish their worth because of their background or circumstances. Together, we faced each challenge as a united front, drawing strength from our bond as a family.

As my daughters grew older, they continued to excel despite the odds stacked against them. They received specialized tutoring that helped them overcome their individual challenges and learning disabilities. With unwavering love and advocacy, I wanted to pave the way for my daughters to carve out their own paths and defy the limitations others tried to impose on them.

Their journey was a testament to the power of resilience, love, and determination in the face of adversity. They have emerged stronger and more united, our bond as a family unshakable despite the challenges we have overcome together. Hopefully, our story becomes an inspiration to others facing similar struggles, showing that with courage and perseverance, anything is possible.

As the years passed, we continued to navigate life's challenges with resilience and determination. Despite the obstacles we faced, both of my daughters graduated from high school with honors, a testament to their hard work and the unwavering support from family and friends. I beamed with pride as I watched my daughters walk across the stage, knowing they had overcome so much to reach this milestone.

I found a new sense of purpose. In my spare time, I pursued my passion for entrepreneurship, dreaming of starting my own business one day. My experiences as a single mother had ignited a fire within me to help others facing similar challenges.

Driven by a desire to make a difference, I began sharing my story with other single mothers in my community. I want to speak at local events and workshops, offering practical advice and emotional support to those navigating solo parenting. I want to encourage them to tap into the strength they gained from their love for their children, reminding them that they are capable of overcoming any obstacle that comes their way.

I want to resonate deeply with those who will listen, sparking hope and determination in the hearts of single mothers who feel alone or overwhelmed. I desire to become a beacon of hope, showing others that with resilience, perseverance, and the support of a loving community, they can create a brighter future for themselves and their children.

I continue to cheer for my girls from the sidelines, proud of the independent and strong young women they have become. Our bond as a family has grown stronger with each passing day, a testament to the love and unity that has carried us through our toughest moments.

Through it all, I will never forget the lessons I have learned on my journey as a single mother. I will remain committed to empowering others and sharing my story as a guide for those facing similar struggles. My dream of becoming an entrepreneur continues to burn brightly, fueled by the belief that I can create opportunities not only for myself but for others in my community.

My story is a testament to the power of love, resilience, and determination in overcoming adversity. It is my hope that my journey from hardship to empowerment inspires countless others, leaving a legacy of hope and strength for generations to come. As I look toward the future, I know that my greatest achievement lies not in the challenges that I have faced, but in the courage that I have shown to my daughters and other supporters along the way.

Chapter 1

Solo Parenting

In this book, I share a message of empowerment and resilience with women who find themselves navigating the challenges of single parenthood. Drawing from my own experiences and lessons learned, I offer practical advice and encouragement. To my readers:

1. Embrace Your Strength: I emphasize the importance of recognizing and embracing the inner strength that every single mother possesses. I encourage readers to tap into this strength during difficult times, reminding them that they are capable of overcoming obstacles and creating a fulfilling life for themselves and their children.

2. Build a Support Network: Understanding the value of support, I encourage readers to build a strong support

network of friends, family, and community resources. I share strategies for reaching out for help when needed and fostering relationships that provide emotional and practical support.

3. Prioritize Self-Care: My book emphasizes the importance of self-care for single mothers, acknowledging that caring for oneself is essential to effectively caring for others. I also offer tips on carving out time for relaxation, hobbies, and personal growth amidst the demands of parenting.

4. Navigate Challenges with Resilience: Reflecting on my own journey, I discuss how to navigate challenges with resilience and determination. I share practical strategies for problem-solving, managing finances, and advocating for one's children in various settings, including school and healthcare.

5. Celebrate Victories, Big and Small: I encourage readers to celebrate their achievements, no matter how small they may seem. I remind them to acknowledge their progress and successes, affirming that every step forward is a testament to their resilience and courage.

6. Inspire Hope for the Future: Above all, I hope that this book is a beacon of hope for single mothers, offering tips of triumph and inspiration. My vision is

of a future where every solo parent can thrive, empowered by love, resilience, and the unwavering belief in their own strength.

An Overview: Understanding Solo Parenting

Being a solo parent is a unique and rewarding experience, filled with its own set of challenges and triumphs. If you're a solo parent, you're not alone—according to the US Census Bureau, over 13 million parents in the United States are raising their children without a partner.

What Is Solo Parenting?

Solo parenting is the act of raising one or more children on your own, without the support of a partner or co-parent. This situation can arise from a variety of circumstances, such as:

- Divorce or separation
- The death of a partner
- Never having been in a relationship
- Choosing to raise a child on your own

No matter the reason, solo parenting requires a lot of hard work, dedication, and resilience.

The Challenges of Solo Parenting

Solo parenting comes with its own set of challenges, including:

- Financial strain: Raising a child on a single income can be difficult, and solo parents often face financial stress and hardship.

- Emotional burden: Solo parents may feel overwhelmed, isolated, and exhausted from shouldering all the responsibilities of parenting on their own.

- Lack of support: Without a partner to share the load, solo parents may feel like they don't have anyone to turn to for help or support.

- Balancing work and parenting: Solo parents often have to balance a job or career with the demands of parenting, which can be a difficult juggling act.

The Triumphs of Solo Parenting

Despite the challenges, solo parenting can also be incredibly rewarding. Here are some of the triumphs of solo parenting:

- Building a strong bond with your child: It is great to know that you have the opportunity to build a deep and meaningful bond with your child, free from the influence of a partner. My daughters and I are very close. They are adults now, and we are great friends.

- Developing resilience and independence: Being resilient and independent, can help you grow as a person and become a stronger parent, even though it can feel lonely at times.

- Creating your own parenting style: I had the freedom to create my own parenting style and make decisions that were best for me and my children.

- Finding support in unexpected places: While it may feel like you're on your own, there is support and community in unexpected places, such as other single parents, friends, and family members. I reached out to family on many occasions.

Everyone understands that parenting on your own is challenging but can be a rewarding experience that requires a lot of hard work and dedication. However, if you understand the challenges and triumphs of solo parenting, you can navigate this journey with confidence. If you get anything out of reading this guide, remember, you're not alone—there is a community of solo parents out there who understand what you're going through and are here to support you. Do not be afraid of reaching out. You do not have to go it alone.

Chapter 2

Stigmas

As if things are not difficult enough, solo parenting comes with a stigma that can be difficult to navigate. This stigma is often perpetuated by societal stereotypes and misconceptions about single parents and their families.

Societal Stereotypes

Single parents are often stereotyped as being irresponsible, promiscuous, or unable to maintain a stable relationship. These stereotypes can be harmful and can contribute to the stigma surrounding single parenthood. These stereotypes are not based in reality because single parents come from all walks of life, with a wide range of experiences, backgrounds, and reasons for becoming a single parent. Every situation is unique and should not be judged.

Misconceptions about Single-Parent Families

There are also many misconceptions about single-parent families. For example, some people believe that children from single-parent homes are more likely to experience behavioral problems, struggle academically, or have difficulty forming healthy relationships. However, research has shown that these assumptions are not necessarily true. In fact, many children from single-parent homes thrive and go on to lead successful, fulfilling lives. I believe this to be true. Perhaps these children have an added willingness to succeed.

The Impact of Stigma

The stigma surrounding single parenthood can have a negative impact on single parents and their children. It can lead to feelings of isolation, shame, and low self-esteem. When people feel shamed as single parents, it becomes more difficult to access the resources and support needed to thrive.

Breaking the Stigma

We all can help to breaking the stigma surrounding single parenthood. Doing so starts with education and awareness. By challenging stereotypes and misconceptions, and by highlighting the strengths and successes of single-parent families, we can help to create a more inclusive and supportive society. People should not have to feel abandoned or ashamed.

Here are some ways to help break the stigma:

- Speak out against stereotypes and misconceptions when you hear them. Do not follow the narrative.

- Share your own experiences as a single parent, and encourage others to do the same.

- Seek out and share positive stories and representations of single-parent families in the media.

- Connect with other single parents and build a supportive community.

- Advocate for policies and resources that support single parents and their families.

The stigma of single parenthood is a complex issue, but by working together to challenge stereotypes and misconceptions. Here again, we can help to create a more inclusive and supportive society for single parents and their families. Remember, being a single parent is nothing to be ashamed of—it's a brave and rewarding experience that comes with its own unique set of challenges and triumphs. I certainly have had many challenges and pushing through them, has made me a stronger person than I ever thought that I could be.

Chapter 3

Emotional Struggles

Emotional struggles are do to the many challenges that are faced as a single parent. In order to maintain your mental and emotional well-being, you must be aware of these challenges. As you are providing a stable and loving environment for your child, do not neglect your mental health. Here are some common emotional struggles faced by single parents, along with some strategies for coping with them.

Grief and Loss

The end of a relationship, whether through divorce or separation, or non-compliant, can bring about feelings of grief and loss. This is a normal and natural response to the end of a significant relationship, or a one-sided relationship. It's important to allow yourself to feel and process these emotions. Here are some tips for coping with grief and loss:

- Allow yourself to feel and process your emotions. Don't try to suppress or ignore them. While going through this ordeal, I did not mind allowing myself to be in my feelings, or to drop tears.

- Seek support from friends, family, or a therapist. Talking about your feelings can help you process them and move forward.

- Take care of yourself physically. Eat a healthy diet, get plenty of sleep, and exercise regularly.

- Practice self-compassion. Be kind and understanding with yourself as you navigate this difficult time.

Isolation and Loneliness

Single parents can sometimes feel isolated and lonely, especially if they don't have a strong support network. This can be challenging even if you're a single parent by choice, or if you've moved to a new area and don't know many people. Here are some tips for coping with isolation and loneliness:

- Unless you would prefer to go through it alone, reach out to friends, family, or support groups for single parents.

- By joining a club or group that interests you, it can be a great way to meet new people.

- Practice self-care. Take time for yourself, even if it's just a few minutes each day. This can help you feel more connected to yourself and less lonely.

Anxiety and Worry

Single parents often worry about their children and their ability to provide for them. This can lead to feelings of anxiety and worry, which can be overwhelming at times. This was the case for me. I had to get a job, a better job. I always worried about being the provided on a limited budget. Here are some tips for coping with anxiety and worry:

- Practice mindfulness or meditation. This can help you stay present and focused, rather than getting caught up in worries about the future.

- Break tasks down into smaller, more manageable steps. This can help you feel more in control and less overwhelmed.

- Seek support from a therapist or support group. Talking about your worries can help. If necessary keep seeking better job opportunities. I understand that childcare can be the determining factor on how work plays a role.

Guilt and Self-Blame

Feeling guilty or blaming yourself for your situation? This can be especially true if you're a single parent by choice, or if you feel like you've failed in some way. However, being a single parent doesn't make you a bad parent. Here are some tips for coping with guilt and self-blame:

- Practice self-compassion. Be kind and understanding with yourself. Everyone makes mistakes, and somethings are not within our control. Remember that you're doing the best you can.

- Seek support from a therapist or support group. Talking about your feelings can help you process them and find a more balanced perspective.

- Focus on the positive. Make a list of the things you're doing well as a parent and the things you're grateful for. This can help shift your focus away from guilt and self-blame.

Emotional struggles are a normal part of life and being a single parent is no exception. By acknowledging and addressing these struggles, you can maintain your mental and emotional well-being, and provide a loving and stable environment for your child.

Chapter 4

Feeling Overwhelmed as a Single Parent

As a single parent, you may often feel overwhelmed with the responsibilities of raising your child or children on your own. This is completely normal and I have been there. I liked closing my eyes for five minutes at a time and taking deep breaths. Here are some tips and strategies to help you manage feelings of overwhelm:

Recognize the Signs of Overwhelm

It's important to be aware of the signs of feeling overwhelmed, which can include:

- Increased stress and anxiety
- Difficulty sleeping
- Irritability or mood swings
- Difficulty concentrating
- Feelings of helplessness or hopelessness

By recognizing these signs, you can take action to address them before they become unmanageable.

Prioritize Self-Care

Taking care of yourself is essential when you're a single parent. Make sure to prioritize self-care activities such as exercise, meditation, and hobbies. This can help reduce stress and increase your overall well-being.

Seek Support

I will repeat this often because it is essential to a healthy state of mind. Don't be afraid to reach out for help and support. Whether it's from family, friends, or a professional therapist, having a support system can make a big difference in managing feelings of overwhelm.

Create a Routine

Establishing a daily routine can help provide structure and predictability in your life. This can help reduce feelings of overwhelm by giving you a clear plan for each day.

Practice Mindfulness

Mindfulness practices such as deep breathing and meditation can help reduce stress and anxiety. Try incorporating these practices into your daily routine.

Break Tasks Down into Smaller Steps

Feeling overwhelmed can often come from facing a large task or responsibility. Breaking tasks down into smaller, manageable steps can help make them feel less daunting. I had to take one day at a time. Sometimes one moment at a time.

Practice Gratitude

Focusing on the positive aspects of your life and practicing gratitude can help shift your mindset and reduce feelings of overwhelm. Try keeping a gratitude journal or sharing what you're grateful for with a loved one. My daughters brought me so much happiness. I felt honored to have them in my life and to be able to care for them. My girls are young women now. I can't say that it is easier for moms today, but there maybe more opportunity to seek help.

So, it's okay to feel overwhelmed. Recognize the signs, prioritize self-care, seek support, create a routine, practice mindfulness, break tasks down, and practice gratitude. Manage these feelings and thrive as a solo parent.

Chapter 5

Dealing with Loneliness as a Single Parent

As a single parent, you may often find yourself feeling lonely or isolated. I was in my marriage and felt lonely as well. The feeling is normal, but it's important to address it in a healthy way. Here are some tips for dealing with loneliness as a single parent. I found comfort in reading books and doing projects with my girls.

Acknowledge Your Feelings

The first step in dealing with loneliness is to acknowledge how you're feeling. It's okay to feel lonely, and recognizing this emotion is the first step in addressing it.

Build a Support System

Reach out to family, friends, and other single parents. If you join a single-parent support group, you may be able to can connect with others who are going through similar experiences. Sometimes meeting new friends can be medicine to the soul.

Schedule Social Activities

Make an effort to schedule social activities with friends and family. Whether it's a weekly coffee date or a monthly game night, having something to look forward to can help combat feelings of loneliness. I loved giving parties for my girls. The parties made me feel appreciated and them feel special.

Practice Self-Care

Taking care of yourself is essential. Prioritizing self-care with activities such as exercise, meditation, and hobbies can combat loneliness. Getting out in nature reminded me that their is life dancing all around us.

Seek Professional Help

If feelings of loneliness persist, and you feel overwhelmed consider reaching out to a therapist or counselor for additional support and guidance. They would have tools to help you process your feelings.

Remember, it's okay to feel lonely as a single parent, but it's important to take action to address these feelings. Build a support system, schedule social activities, practice self-care, and seek professional help when necessary.

Chapter 6

Financial Challenges

Being a single parent can be financially challenging. According to the US Census Bureau, in 2019, there were 11.8 million single-parent families in the United States, and they were more likely to live in poverty than married-couple families. As a single parent, you are solely responsible for providing for your family's needs, which can be overwhelming. However, with careful planning and budgeting, you can overcome financial challenges and provide a stable life for your children.

Understanding Your Income and Expenses

As a single parent understand your income and expenses. Make a list of all your sources of income, including your salary, child support, and any government assistance you receive. Then, make a list of all your expenses, including housing, food, transportation, child care, health insurance, and any outstanding debts. This was hard for me at first as I did not want to take be accountable for my spending.

Once you have a clear picture of your income and expenses, you can create a budget. Allocate a portion of your income to each expense, making sure to prioritize essential needs such as housing, food, and child care. It's essential to stick to your budget as much as possible, but don't be too hard on yourself if you slip up occasionally.

Reducing Expenses

There are many ways to reduce your expenses as a single parent. Here are some tips:

- Cook meals at home instead of eating out or ordering takeout.

- Use coupons and shop sales when buying groceries and other essentials.

- Cancel any subscriptions or memberships you don't use frequently.

- Shop secondhand for clothes and household items.

- Use public transportation or carpool when possible to save on gas and car maintenance costs.

- Consider downsizing to a smaller home or apartment to save on housing costs.

Increasing Your Income

In addition to reducing expenses, increasing your income can also help you overcome financial challenges as a single parent. Here are some ideas:

- Ask for a raise or promotion at work. I changed jobs.

- Consider taking on a side hustle, such as freelancing or consulting.

- Sell unwanted items online or at a yard sale.

- Look for government assistance programs for single parents, such as food assistance or housing subsidies.

Saving for the Future

As a single parent, it's essential to save for the future. Here are some tips:

- Set aside a portion of your income in a savings account.

- Consider investing in a retirement account, such as a 401(k) or IRA.

- Save for your children's education by setting up a college savings plan.

- Create an emergency fund to cover unexpected expenses.

Seeking Support

Finally, don't be afraid to seek support when needed. Consider seeking financial advice from a professional. Remember, there are resources available to help you overcome financial challenges as a single parent.

Chapter 7

Managing a Single-Income Household

Managing a single-income household can be challenging. However, it can be possible to create a stable and secure financial life for you and your children.

Create a Realistic Budget

Create a realistic budget which includes tracking your income and expenses, and determining how much money you have available for necessary expenses such as housing, food, transportation, and healthcare.

When creating your budget, be sure to include savings as a priority. Even if it's a small amount each month, setting aside money for emergencies and future goals can help provide financial security and stability.

Prioritize Necessary Expenses

Do not forget that it's important to prioritize necessary expenses such as housing, food, transportation, and healthcare. These expenses should be paid first, before discretionary expenses such as entertainment and travel.

It may be necessary to take steps towards downsizing your housing or finding ways to reduce your transportation costs, such as carpooling or using public transportation. Look for ways to save on food expenses, such as meal planning, cooking at home, and buying in bulk.

Seek Out Assistance

There are many resources available for single parents, including government assistance programs, non-profit organizations, and community resources.

Increase Your Income

Consider taking on a part-time job, freelancing, or starting a side hustle.

Look for opportunities to increase your skills and education, which can lead to higher-paying jobs in the future. Consider taking online courses or attending workshops to improve your skills and knowledge.

By following these tips, you can manage a single-income household as a single parent and create a stable and secure financial life for you and your children. Remember, it's possible to thrive as a single parent, and with careful planning and prioritizing, you can achieve your financial goals and build a bright future for your family.

Chapter 8

Savings, Insurance, and Retirement

Planning for the future is essential to ensure the well-being and stability of yourself and your children. I will cover three crucial areas of future planning: savings, insurance, and retirement.

Savings

1. Emergency Fund

An emergency fund is a crucial first step in your savings plan. Aim to save at least three to six months 'worth of living expenses to cover unexpected costs, such as car repairs or medical bills. This fund should be easily accessible and kept in a high-yield savings account or a money market account.

2. Short-Term Savings

Short-term savings are for planned expenses that will occur within the next one to five years, such as a car purchase, home repairs, or your children's education expenses. It is helpful to use a separate savings account specifically for these goals and contribute to it regularly.

3. Long-Term Savings

Long-term savings are for expenses that will occur beyond five years, like retirement or your children's college education. Investing in a diversified portfolio, including stocks, bonds, and mutual funds, will grow your savings over time.

Insurance

1. Health Insurance

Not every country has free health insurance. Investigate options through your employer, the marketplace, or Medicaid/Medicare.

2. Life Insurance

Life insurance can provide financial security for your children in case of your untimely demise. A term life insurance policy with a coverage amount that will cover your children's expenses until they are financially independent is a great option. Term life insurance is less expensive to start with. Whole life can be more costly.

3. Disability Insurance

Disability insurance can replace a portion of your income if you become unable to work due to illness or injury. A long-term disability insurance policy can protect your income and your family's financial future.

4. Home and Auto Insurance

Home and auto insurance protect your assets in case of damage or liability. Make sure you have adequate coverage and consider bundling policies to save on premiums.

Retirement

1. 401(k) or 403(b) Plan

If your employer offers a 401(k) or 403(b) plan, contribute as much as possible, especially if your employer matches your contributions. Matched programs are a game changer for growing your nest egg. I was fortunate that my job offered a matched savings plan.

2. IRA

If you don't have access to an employer-sponsored plan, consider opening an Individual Retirement Account (IRA). Contributions to a traditional IRA may be tax-deductible, and both traditional and Roth IRAs provide tax-deferred growth. Do your research and learn as much as you can about the different retirement plans.

3. Social Security

As a single parent, you may be eligible for Social Security benefits, including survivor benefits for your children. Make sure to create a "my Social Security" account to keep track of your earnings and benefits.

This is a lot to consider, but it is necessary to be informed. Do not worry about trying to do all of these plans at once, but know that they are available. By following these steps, you can create a solid plan for your family's financial future. Remember, planning for the future is an ongoing process, and it's essential to review and adjust your plan as your circumstances change.

Chapter 9

Time Management

Do we ever have enough time. I don't think that there is enough time in a day, but we have to work with what we have been given. Here are some tips and strategies to help you make the most of your time:

Create a Schedule

- Establish a daily routine for you and your children.
- Include regular times for meals, homework, chores, and play.

- Use a planner or calendar to keep track of appointments and deadlines.
- Color-code activities for each family member to stay organized.

Prioritize Tasks

- Make a to-do list of tasks that need to be accomplished.
- Rank tasks in order of importance.
- Allocate time for each task and stick to the schedule.
- Delegate tasks to your children when appropriate.

Set Realistic Goals

- Set achievable goals for yourself and your children.
- Break larger goals into smaller, manageable tasks.
- Celebrate accomplishments to build confidence and motivation.

Limit Distractions

- Turn off electronic devices during designated times.
- Create a quiet workspace for homework and work tasks.
- Limit extracurricular activities to a reasonable number.
- As always, ask for help when needed to avoid feeling overwhelmed.

Make Time for Yourself

- As always, schedule regular self-care activities.
- Prioritize exercise, meditation, or hobbies.
- Again, seek support from friends, family, or a therapist.
- Remember that taking care of yourself is essential for taking care of your children.

When you implement time management strategies, you can reduce stress, increase productivity, and create a more balanced and fulfilling life for yourself and your children.

I enjoyed getting up a little earlier and getting certain task completed. I became more focused during the rest of the day. It was clarifying for me. For example, gardening relaxed me and I got a job done.

Chapter 10

Balancing Work and Parenting as a Single Parent

Finding a healthy balance between work and parenting can often feel like a daunting task. Here are some tips and strategies to help you maintain this balance and thrive in both aspects of your life.

Establish a Routine

Creating a daily and weekly routine can help you manage your time more effectively. Include specific times for work tasks, household chores, and quality time with your children. Make sure to also allocate time for relaxation.

Set Boundaries

Depending on your job or profession, you may have to set clear boundaries between your work and personal life. Maintain balance by communicating your work schedule and availability to your employer and coworkers. Try to avoid bringing work-related tasks into your personal time. Leave work and work!

Seek Support

Don't hesitate to ask for help and support when needed. Reach out to others who can provide assistance with child care, household tasks, or emotional support. Again, joining single-parent support groups or online communities for additional resources and encouragement.

Prioritize and Organize

Make a list of your most important tasks, responsibilities, and goals. Prioritize them based on their urgency and importance. Sometimes working with time management tools, such as calendars, planners, or productivity apps, can be work. However, many of them can help you stay organized and focused.

Consider Flexible Work Arrangements

Flexible work options are on the rise. Your employer may be able to offer you remote work, flextime, or a compressed workweek. These arrangements can help you better balance your work and parenting responsibilities while providing a more flexible schedule.

Embrace Imperfection

Understand that achieving a perfect balance between work and parenting is not realistic. Instead, focus on creating a harmonious environment where your needs and the needs of your children are met. Embrace the imperfections and celebrate the small victories.

Create Quality Time

Plan intentional, high-quality activities with your children. Engage in conversations, share stories, and enjoy hobbies together. These moments can help strengthen your bond and create lasting memories.

Engage in Self-Care and Personal Growth

This is easier said than done. Make self-care a priority by dedicating time for relaxation, exercise, and personal growth. I am always trying to improve on self-care. Practicing mindfulness, engaging in meditation, or enjoying hobbies can help reduce stress, increase energy levels, and improve overall well-being.

Think about Financial Planning

As stated above, manage your finances wisely to ensure stability and reduce financial stress. Create a budget, save for emergencies, and explore resources for single parents, such as financial assistance programs or child support services.

Use Open Communication

Maintain open and honest communication with your children about your work and parenting responsibilities. Explain your schedule, discuss any changes, and involve them in decision-making processes. This can help them better understand your situation and foster a stronger relationship.

Balancing work and parenting as a single parent can be challenging, but with the right strategies and support, you can achieve this.

Chapter 11

Self-Care and Personal Time

Many parents forget about taking care of themselves while managing the responsibilities of raising children alone. However, self-care is not a luxury; it's a necessity. I worried myself often. I know now that worrying was not healthy. I hope that this guide will enlighten you and help you on your journey.

The Importance of Self-Care

Self-care is essential for maintaining your physical, mental, and emotional well-being. By taking care of yourself, you'll be better equipped to model healthy behaviors for your children.

Making Time for Self-Care

Finding time for self-care can be challenging, but it's crucial to prioritize it. Here are some tips for incorporating self-care into your daily routine:

1. Schedule It In

Treat self-care like any other appointment or commitment. Put it on your calendar and make it non-negotiable.

2. Start Small

Begin with small, manageable self-care activities, such as taking a 10-minute walk or enjoying a cup of tea in silence. As you become more comfortable with self-care, you can gradually increase the length and intensity of your activities.

3. Get Creative

Self-care does n't have to be expensive or time-consuming. I enjoy activities that bring peace, such as reading, painting, or gardening.

4. Ask for Help

Don't be afraid to ask for help from friends, family. Delegating tasks can free up time for self-care. At the beginning of my solo journey, I depended on my family for help.

Personal Time

Personal time is time spent alone, without any distractions or obligations. It's an opportunity to recharge, reflect, and pursue personal interests. Here are some tips for making the most of your personal time:

1. Unplug

Turn off your phone, computer, and other electronic devices. Use this time to disconnect from the digital world and connect with yourself.

2. Explore New Hobbies

Use your personal time to try new activities and hobbies. This can help you discover new passions and interests, as well as provide a sense of accomplishment and fulfillment. I now that this can be a chore for many moms, but I enjoy learning new recipes.

3. Reflect

Use your personal time to reflect on your goals, values, and priorities. This can help you stay grounded and focused on what truly matters.

4. Practice Gratitude

Take a few moments to reflect on the things you're grateful for. This can help shift your focus from stress and negativity to positivity and happiness.

Remember, self-care and personal time are not selfish or indulgent. They're essential for maintaining your physical, mental, and emotional well-being. As a single parent, taking care of yourself is an important part of taking care of your child.

Chapter 12

Building Strong Bonds

As a single parent, building a strong bond with your child is crucial. It not only helps to create a stable and loving environment for your child, but also contributes to their emotional, social, and cognitive development. Here are some tips and strategies to help you build and strengthen your bond with your child:

1. Spend Quality Time Together

Make time for activities that you and your child can enjoy together. This could be as simple as reading a book together before bedtime, cooking a meal, or going for a walk. The goal is to create opportunities for meaningful conversations and shared experiences.

2. Listen Actively and Empathically

Listening to your child is one of the most important ways to build a strong bond. When they speak, give them your undivided attention, and show empathy toward their feelings and experiences. This helps them feel valued, understood, and loved.

3. Express Your Love and Affection

Don't hesitate to express your love and affection toward your child. Show them physical affection, such as hugs, kisses, and cuddles, and tell them often that you love them. These small gestures can have a big impact on their emotional well-being. I loved on my girls as often as I could.

4. Establish Consistent Routines

Having consistent routines can help your child feel secure and loved. Whether it's a bedtime routine, a morning routine, or a weekly family day, routines provide a sense of stability and predictability that can strengthen your bond.

5. Encourage Independence and Self-Esteem

Encourage your child to be independent and make their own decisions. This helps to build their self-esteem and confidence. Be there to support them when they make mistakes, and use these moments as opportunities for learning and growth.

6. Create a Positive Home Environment

Creating a positive and nurturing home environment can help to build strong confidence in your child. This means providing a safe and loving space where they can express themselves freely, without fear of judgment or criticism.

7. Seek Out Support and Resources

Building strong bonds with your child could include joining a single-parent support group, attending parenting classes, or seeking counseling or therapy. Remember, you don't have to do it alone.

By implementing these tips and strategies, you can build and strengthen your bond with your child, creating a foundation for a happy and healthy relationship. I was diligent about bonding with my girls and letting them know how much they meant to me.

Chapter 13

Nurturing Emotional Connection

One of the most important things you can do for your child is to nurture a strong emotional connection with them. This connection will provide a foundation for your relationship, helping your child feel loved, secure, and supported. Here are some tips for nurturing an emotional connection with your child:

Be Present and Engaged

When you are with your child, be fully present and engaged. I know that this is difficult, as there are so many things pulling us in different directions. However, try to put away your phone and other distractions, and focus on your child. Listen to them, ask questions, and show interest in what they are saying and doing. This will help your child feel valued and important, and it will strengthen your emotional connection.

Show Empathy and Understanding

When your child is upset or going through a difficult time, show empathy and understanding. Try to see things from their perspective and let them know that you understand how they are feeling. This will help your child feel heard and supported.

Spend Quality Time Together

Spending quality time together is a great way to nurture connections with your child. This doesn't have to mean doing anything elaborate or expensive. Going for a walk, or playing a game can be meaningful. The important thing is to spend time together where you can focus on each other and build your relationship. Besides giving great parties for my girls, I loved reading to them.

Express Your Love and Affection

Don't be afraid to express your love and affection for your child. Tell them that you love them, hug them, and show physical affection. This will help your child feel loved and secure.

Be a Role Model

As a single parent, you are your child's primary role model. Show them what it means to have a strong emotional connection by nurturing your own relationships and taking care of your own emotional well-being. This will help your child learn how to build and maintain connections in their own relationships.

Nurturing an emotional connection with your child is an ongoing process, but it is one that is well worth the effort. My daughters have grown up, but they know that they can share their concerns with me anytime. I am available for them. I stay present in their lives. By being present, engaged, empathetic, and loving, you can build a strong foundation for your relationship with your child that will last a lifetime.

Chapter 14

Quality Time

It's crucial to make an effort to create special moments. Here are some tips on how to engage in quality time with your children as a solo parent:

Schedule It In

With a busy schedule, it's essential to plan and set aside specific times for quality time with your children. Use those calendars in your phone to schedule time for your child.

Be Present

When spending quality time with your children, put away your phone, turn off the TV, and focus on them. Being fully present in the moment will show your children that they are essential and valued.

Ask for Their Input

Involve your children in the planning process by asking them what they would like to do during your quality time together. Giving them a say in the activities will make them more excited and engaged.

Do Something New

Try something new and exciting together, such as visiting a museum, going on a hike, or attending a local event. These experiences will create lasting memories and provide opportunities for learning and growth.

Keep It Simple

Simple activities can be very meaningful and enjoyable. Putting together puzzles or drawing can be rewarding.

Make It Routine

Establish a regular routine for quality time with your children, such as a weekly movie night or a monthly outing. Consistency will help make these moments a cherished tradition.

Be Flexible

Life can be unpredictable, and plans may change. Be open to adjusting your quality time activities to accommodate unexpected events or circumstances.

Enjoy the Moment

Most importantly, have fun and enjoy the time spent with your children. These quality moments will be cherished.

By following these tips, you can create meaningful and memorable experiences with your children as a single parent.

Chapter 15

Developing Resilience as a Single Parent

Single parenting is a challenging journey, but it also provides an opportunity for growth and resilience. Developing resilience can help you navigate the ups and downs of solo parenting and come out stronger on the other side. Here's some information on how to build resilience as a single parent:

Understanding Resilience

Resilience is the ability to bounce back from adversity, trauma, or stress. It's not something that you're born with, but rather a skill that can be developed and strengthened over time.

Building Resilience

Building resilience involves taking care of yourself physically, emotionally, and mentally. Here are some tips for building resilience as a single parent:

1. Practice Self-Care

Self-care is essential for building resilience. Make sure to prioritize self-care activities such as exercise, meditation, and relaxation techniques. Taking care of yourself will help you better manage stress and build the strength you need to handle the challenges of solo parenting.

2. Connect with Others

Connecting with others is also important. Building a strong support network can help you feel less isolated and provide you with the encouragement and assistance you need to navigate the challenges of single parenting.

3. Develop Problem-Solving Skills

Developing problem-solving skills can help you build resilience and handle the challenges of solo parenting. Practice breaking down problems into smaller parts, brainstorming solutions, and implementing a plan of action.

4. Focus on the Positive

Focusing on the positive can help you build resilience and maintain a positive outlook. Practice gratitude, celebrate small victories, and find joy in the everyday moments of solo parenting. Time is going to go by faster than you would expect. Therefore take the moments in with pleasure.

5. Seek Professional Help

If you're struggling to build resilience on your own, a counselor can provide you with guidance, support, and tools to help you build resilience and manage the challenges of solo parenting.

The Benefits of Resilience

Building resilience can include:

- Improved well-being and mental health
- Better stress management
- Increased confidence and self-esteem
- Stronger relationships and support networks
- A greater sense of purpose and meaning in life

By building resilience, you can navigate the challenges of solo parenting with greater ease and confidence. You can be of help to others in your same situations.

Chapter 16

Overcoming Obstacles

Single parenting with its own unique set of challenges and obstacles can seem overwhelming. However, with the right mindset and tools, it is possible to overcome these obstacles as a solo parent.

Financial Challenges

We may all agree that one of the biggest obstacles that single parents face is financial strain. Raising a child on a single income can be difficult, but there are ways to make it work as was stated in previous chapters.

- Budgeting: Creating a budget is essential for managing your finances as a single parent. Track your income and expenses, and make a plan for where your money will go each month.

- Government Assistance: Don't be afraid to seek out government assistance programs that can help you with things like food, housing, and healthcare costs.

- Work-Life Balance: Consider finding a job that offers flexible hours or the ability to work from home. This can help you save on child care costs and give you more time with your child.

Emotional Challenges

The emotional challenges of single parenting can be just as difficult as the financial ones. It's important to take care of your mental health and seek support when needed.

- Self-Care: Make sure to take time for yourself, even if it's just a few minutes each day. This can help you recharge and reduce stress.

- Support System: Surround yourself with a strong support system of friends, family, and other single parents. They can provide emotional support and practical help when needed.

- Therapy: Therapy or counseling can help you navigate the emotional challenges of single parenting.

Social Challenges

Single parents often face social challenges, such as stigma and isolation. It's important to build a strong social network and advocate for yourself and your child.

- Community: Get involved in your community by joining local groups or organizations. This can help you meet other single parents and build a support network.

- Advocacy: Advocate for yourself and your child by speaking up about your needs and concerns. This can help you get the resources and support you need.

- Self-Acceptance: Embrace your role as a single parent and recognize the strength and resilience it takes to raise a child on your own.

Parenting Challenges

Parenting as a single parent can be challenging, but there are ways to make it work.

- Consistency: Establish consistent routines and expectations for your child. This can help them feel secure and build good habits.

- Communication: Keep the lines of communication open with your child. Talk to them about their feelings and concerns, and listen actively.

- Self-Care: Remember to take care of yourself, too. A healthy, happy parent is better able to care for their child.

While single parenting comes with its own unique set of obstacles, it is possible to overcome them with the right mindset and tools. Embrace your role as a single parent. You are strong, capable, and deserving of respect and support.

Chapter 17

Embracing Change as a Single Parent

Change is an inevitable part of life, especially for single parents. The journey is full of transitions and transformations. Embracing change is essential. Try to find happiness in your reality. Here's why:

Change Brings Growth

As single parents, we are constantly evolving and learning new skills. From managing finances to dealing with emotional challenges, change is an opportunity to grow and become a stronger person. Embracing change allows us to adapt and thrive in our roles as a parent.

Change Encourages Flexibility

You need to be flexible to handle whatever comes your way. Embracing change allows you to be open-minded and adaptable, making it easier to navigate the ups and downs of solo parenting. Whether it's a change in your work schedule or your child's needs, being flexible is key to maintaining a positive and healthy family life.

Change Fosters Resilience

Single parenting is full of challenges. By facing changes head-on, you build emotional strength and learn to bounce back from setbacks. This resilience not only benefits you but also sets a positive example for your children, teaching them the importance of perseverance and determination.

Change Promotes Positive Thinking

Embracing change requires a positive attitude and a willingness to see the bright side of things. By focusing on the benefits of change, you can shift your mindset and cultivate a more optimistic outlook. This positive thinking can have a ripple effect, improving your overall well-being and creating a happier home environment for you and your children.

Change Encourages Self-Care

It's easy to put your needs on the back burner. However, embracing change can help you prioritize self-care. Whether it's taking a yoga class or scheduling a weekly date night, self-care is essential for single parents to maintain their physical, emotional, and mental health. By taking care of yourself, you'll be better equipped to handle the challenges of solo parenting and model healthy habits.

In conclusion, embracing change is crucial for single parents to navigate the pains, challenges, and triumphs of solo parenting. By viewing change as an opportunity for growth, fostering flexibility, building resilience, promoting positive thinking, and encouraging self-care, single parents can thrive in their new role and create a happy, healthy home for themselves and their children.

Chapter 18

Celebrate

As single parents, we know that our journey is filled with its fair share of ups and downs. We need to also recognize and celebrate our successes along the way. In this section, we'll dive into the importance of celebrating success and offer some ideas on how to do so.

The Power of Celebrating Success

We often juggle multiple roles, responsibilities, and tasks daily. It's easy to get caught up in our to-do lists and forget to take a moment to appreciate our accomplishments. Here's why celebrating success matters:

1. It Boosts Self-Confidence

Acknowledging our achievements reinforces our belief in our abilities, making us more resilient and better equipped to tackle future challenges.

2. It Encourages Gratitude

Celebrating success allows us to reflect on the support system that helped us get there, fostering a sense of gratitude for our loved ones and the resources available to us.

3. It Promotes Motivation and Positivity

Recognizing our accomplishments keeps us motivated and helps us maintain a positive outlook on our single-parenting journey.

Ideas for Celebrating Success

Now that we understand the benefits of celebrating success, let's explore some ideas to incorporate into our daily lives:

1. Verbalize Your Accomplishments

Take a moment to verbalize your successes, no matter how small. Share them with your children, friends, or family to reinforce their significance.

2. Treat Yourself

Set aside time for self-care or indulge in a special treat as a reward for achieving a goal. This can be as simple as ordering takeout from your favorite restaurant.

3. Create a Victory Jar

Write down your accomplishments on slips of paper and place them in a jar. Periodically, read through the slips to reminisce on your achievements and boost your mood.

4. Share Your Story

Share your successes with others in the solo-parenting community to inspire and support one another. You never know who might benefit from hearing your story!

5. Reflect on Your Growth

Take time to reflect on how far you've come and the progress you've made. This can help put things into perspective and remind you of your resilience.

By incorporating these practices into our daily lives, we can celebrate our successes, build self-confidence, and maintain a positive outlook on our single-parenting journey. Keep up the fantastic work, solo parents—you're doing an amazing job!

Chapter 19

Wins

I now want to talk to you about something super important: acknowledging small wins.

When you're a single parent, life can get pretty hectic. You've got a million and one things on your plate, and it can be tough to keep up with them all. That's why it's so crucial to take a step back and celebrate the little victories along the way.

Here are some tips on how to do just that:

1. Set Realistic Goals

It's important to set goals that are achievable for you and your family. Don't set yourself up for failure by aiming too high. Break your larger goals into smaller, manageable tasks that you can accomplish on a daily or weekly basis.

2. Recognize Your Achievements

When you do complete a task or reach a goal, take a moment to acknowledge it. Give yourself a pat on the back, do a happy dance, or treat yourself to something special (even if it's just a piece of chocolate!).

3. Share Your Successes

Don't be afraid to share your small wins with others. Whether it's your kids, your friends, or your family, let people know when you've accomplished something. Not only will it make you feel good, but it will also inspire others to celebrate their own small wins.

4. Stay Positive

It's easy to get bogged down in the day-to-day struggles of solo parenting, but it's important to stay positive and focus on the good things in your life. When you recognize and celebrate your small wins, you're training your brain to look for the positive aspects of your life.

5. Keep a Victory Journal

One great way to acknowledge your small wins is to keep a victory journal. Every time you accomplish something, write it down in your journal. At the end of the week, read through your victories and bask in the glory of all that you've accomplished.

Remember, being a solo parent is a challenging but rewarding journey. By taking the time to acknowledge your small wins, you'll be better equipped to handle the ups and downs of single parenting. Keep up the good work, and keep on celebrating!

Chapter 20

Goals

As a single parent, setting and achieving goals can be a powerful way to take control of your life and create a better future for your family. By following a few simple steps, you can turn your dreams into reality and become a more confident, capable, and successful parent.

Step 1: Define Your Goals

The first step in setting and achieving goals is to define what you want to accomplish. This may seem obvious, but many people fail to reach their goals because they haven't taken the time to clearly define what they are.

When defining your goals, it's important to make them specific, measurable, achievable, relevant, and time-bound. For example, instead of saying "I want to lose weight," say "I want to lose 10 pounds in the next two months by exercising for 30 minutes a day and eating a healthy diet."

Step 2: Create a Plan

Once you have defined your goals, the next step is to create a plan for achieving them. This should include specific actions you will take, resources you will need, and a timeline for completion.

For example, if your goal is to lose 10 pounds in two months, your plan might include:

- Exercising for 30 minutes a day, five days a week
- Eating a healthy diet that includes plenty of fruits, vegetables, and lean protein
- Tracking your progress in a journal or using a fitness app

- Rewarding yourself for milestones along the way

Step 3: Take Action

With your plan in place, it's time to take action! This is often the hardest part of setting and achieving goals, but it's also the most rewarding.

Remember to focus on one step at a time, and don't get discouraged if you encounter setbacks or obstacles. Instead, use them as learning experiences and adjust your plan as needed.

Step 4: Celebrate Your Successes

Finally, don't forget to celebrate your successes along the way! Achieving goals is a journey, and it's important to recognize and reward yourself for the progress you've made.

This can be as simple as treating yourself to a favorite meal or activity, or it can be something more substantial like a weekend getaway or a new piece of clothing. The important thing is to acknowledge your hard work and celebrate your achievements.

By following these steps, you can set and achieve meaningful goals as a single parent. Whether you're looking to improve your health, advance your career, or create a better life for you and your children, setting and achieving goals can help you get there. So get started today and see what you can accomplish!

Chapter 21

Support Systems

Building a Support Network: A Key to Successful Solo Parenting

It's essential to have a robust support network to help you navigate the challenges of raising children on your own. A support network can provide emotional, practical, and financial assistance, making your journey as a solo parent more manageable and fulfilling. In this section, I will discuss the importance of building a support network and offer tips and strategies for creating and maintaining one.

What Is a Support Network?

A support network is a group of people who provide emotional, practical, and social support to an individual or family. In the context of solo parenting, a support network may include family members, friends, neighbors, colleagues, and other single parents. The network can provide various forms of assistance, such as child care, emotional support, practical help, and advice.

Why Is Building a Support Network Important?

Building a support network is essential for several reasons:

1. It Reduces Stress and Isolation

Parenting can be stressful and isolating. A support network can help reduce stress and feelings of isolation by providing emotional support and companionship.

2. It Provides Practical Help

Single parents often juggle multiple responsibilities, including work, child care, and household tasks. A support network can provide practical help, such as child care, errand-running, and housekeeping, allowing you to focus on other important tasks.

3. It Offers Advice and Guidance

Other single parents and experienced parents can offer advice and guidance on various aspects of solo parenting, such as discipline, education, and self-care.

4. It Enhances Social Connections

A support network can provide opportunities for social connections and activities, helping you and your children build relationships and community connections.

How to Build a Support Network

Building a support network takes time and effort, but the rewards are well worth it. Here are some tips and strategies for creating and maintaining a support network:

1. Identify Your Needs

Before building a support network, identify your needs and priorities. What kind of support do you need? Child care, emotional support, practical help, or advice? Once you know what you need, you can start looking for people who can provide that support.

2. Reach out to Family and Friends

Your family and friends are often the first line of defense when it comes to building a support network. Reach out to them and let them know how they can help. Be specific about your needs and what you would appreciate their assistance with.

3. Join Single-Parent Groups

Single-parent groups can provide a sense of community and support for solo parents. Look for groups in your local area or online and attend meetings or events. These groups can provide opportunities for social connections, advice, and practical help.

4. Connect with Neighbors

Neighbors can be a valuable resource for solo parents. Consider introducing yourself and building relationships with your neighbors. They may be able to provide practical help, such as watching your children or lending a tool, and can be a source of emotional support.

5. Seek Professional Help

If you're struggling to build a support network or are experiencing significant stress or mental health issues, consider seeking professional help. Building a support network and managing stress.

6. Maintain Your Support Network

Building a support network is just the beginning. It's essential to maintain your network by staying in touch with your supporters, expressing gratitude, and offering help in return. Consider hosting social events, sending thank-you notes, and offering assistance when you can.

In conclusion, building a support network is crucial for successful solo parenting. A support network can provide emotional, practical, and social support, reducing stress and isolation and enhancing social connections. By identifying your needs, reaching out to family and friends, joining single-parent groups, connecting with neighbors, seeking professional help, and maintaining your network, you can create a robust and supportive community for yourself and your children.

Chapter 22

Family and Friends

As a single parent, you don't have to go it alone. One of the most important things you can do for yourself and your children is to build a strong support network of friends and family. Here's why:

Sharing the Load

Having a network of people you can rely on can help lighten the load. Friends and family can help with child care, transportation, errands, and more. This can give you some much-needed breaks.

Emotional Support

Parenting can be challenging, and it's important to have people you can talk to about your struggles and successes. Friends and family can provide emotional support, encouragement, and a listening ear. They can also offer a fresh perspective and helpful advice when you need it.

Socialization for Your Children

When you have friends and family who are involved in your children's lives, it can provide additional opportunities for socialization and connection. This can be especially important when you do not have as much time to devote to building your children's social networks.

How to Build Your Support Network

Building a support network takes time and effort, but it's worth it. Here are some tips for getting started:

1. Identify Your Needs

Think about the areas where you need the most support. Do you need help with child care or transportation? Do you need someone to talk to about the challenges of single parenting? Once you know what you need, you can start looking for people who can help.

2. Reach Out!

Don't be afraid to reach out to friends and family for help. Most people are happy to lend a hand, but they may not know how to offer their support. Be specific about what you need and when you need it.

3. Join a Support Group

Consider joining a support group for single parents. This can be a great way to connect with other people who are going through similar experiences. You can find support groups online or in your local community.

4. Build Relationships with Other Parents

Get to know other parents in your community. This can be a great way to build a support network and find people who can relate to your experiences. You can meet other parents at school events, sports games, or through community organizations.

5. Prioritize Self-Care

When you're feeling overwhelmed, it's important to have people you can turn to for support. Make sure to prioritize self-care and build a support network that can help you maintain your physical and emotional well-being.

Building a support network of friends and family can be a game-changer for single parents. By sharing the load, providing emotional support, and giving your children opportunities to socialize, you can create a strong foundation for yourself and your family. So don't be afraid to reach out and ask for help. You're not alone. There are people who care about you and your children.

Chapter 23

Connecting with Other Single Parents

Being a single parent can be an incredibly challenging experience. There are millions of other single parents out there who are going through the same things as you. Other single parents can provide a sense of community, support, and understanding that can be invaluable during the tough times.

Benefits of Connecting with Other Single Parents

There are many benefits to connecting with other single parents, including:

- Shared Experiences: Other single parents can provide a unique perspective on the challenges you're facing, as they've likely been through similar situations themselves.

- Emotional Support: Talking to other single parents can help you feel less isolated and provide a much-needed emotional outlet.

- Practical Help: Other single parents may be able to offer practical help, such as sharing tips and resources, or even providing child care assistance in a pinch.

- Access to Role Models: Seeing other single parents thrive can provide inspiration and motivation for your own journey.

Ways to Connect with Other Single Parents

There are many ways to connect with other single parents, both online and in person. Do some research and find communities in your area. Here are a few ideas:

1. Online Communities

There are many forums, social media groups, and blogs online. These communities can provide a safe space to connect with other single parents, ask questions, and share experiences.

2. Local Groups

There may be local groups in your area for single parents, such as support groups or social clubs. These groups can provide a great opportunity to meet other single parents in person and build a sense of community.

- Meetup (https://www.meetup.com/)
- Single Parents Network (https://www.singleparentsnetwork.org/)

3. Events

There are many events for single parents, such as workshops, conferences, and retreats. These events can provide a great opportunity to learn new skills, connect with other single parents, and have some fun.

4. Volunteering

Volunteering can be a great way to meet other single parents while also giving back to your community. Look for volunteer opportunities with organizations that focus on families or children, such as schools, libraries, or community centers.

5. Making Connections

Once you've connected with other single parents, it's important to nurture those relationships. Here are a few tips:

- Be open and honest about your experiences and challenges.
- Offer support and encouragement to other single parents.
- Be willing to listen and provide a sounding board for other single parents.

- Don't be afraid to ask for help or advice when you need it.

Connecting with other single parents can be a powerful tool for navigating the pains, challenges, and triumphs of solo parenting. Whether you're connecting online or in person, remember that you're not alone and that there is a whole community of single parents out there who understand what you're going through.

Chapter 24

Government Assistance

There are many resources available to help make your journey a little bit easier. Here are some ways you can utilize resources as a single parent.

Canada

Resources available for single mothers living in Canada:

Financial Assistance

- Canada Child Benefit (CCB):

- Description: A tax-free monthly payment made to eligible families to help with the cost of raising children under 18 years of age.
- Website: canada.ca/en/revenue-agency/services/child-family-benefits/canada-child-benefit-overview.html

- Goods and Services Tax/Harmonized Sales Tax (GST/HST) Credit:
    - Description: A tax-free quarterly payment that helps individuals and families with low incomes offset all or part of the GST or HST they pay.
    - Website: canada.ca/en/revenue-agency/services/child-family-benefits/goods-services-tax-harmonized-sales-tax-gst-hst-credit.html

- Provincial and Territorial Benefits:
    - Description: Each province and territory offers additional financial support programs for families and children.
    - Website: Varies by province and territory

Employment and Education

- Canada Job Bank:
  - Description: Offers job search tools, career planning, and job matching services.
  - Website: jobbank.gc.ca/home
- Employment Insurance (EI) for Single Parents:
  - Description: Provides temporary financial assistance to unemployed Canadians while they look for work or upgrade their skills.
  - Website: canada.ca/en/employment-social-development/programs/ei/ei-list/reports/maternity-parental.html

Child Care Support

- Child Care Subsidy Programs:
  - Description: Provincial and territorial programs that offer financial assistance to help with child care costs.
  - Website: Varies by province and territory (e.g., Ontario Child Care Subsidy: ontario.ca/page/child-care-subsidies)

Housing Support

- Affordable Housing Programs:
  - Description: Federal, provincial, and municipal programs that provide access to affordable housing.
  - Website: cmhc-schl.gc.ca

Health and Wellness

- Provincial and Territorial Health Plans:
  - Description: Provide access to essential healthcare services.
  - Website: Varies by province and territory (e.g., Ontario Health Insurance Plan (OHIP): ontario.ca/page/apply-ohip-and-get-health-card)
- Mental Health Support:
  - Description: Access to counseling, therapy, and support groups for single mothers.
  - Website: cmha.ca

Legal Assistance

- Legal Aid Services
    - Description: Offers legal assistance for low-income individuals, including family law support.
    - Website: Varies by province and territory (e.g., Legal Aid Ontario: legalaid.on.ca)

Community Support

- Single-Parent Support Groups:
    - Description: Community organizations and online groups that provide support and resources.
    - Example: singlemothersinprogress.com
- Food Banks and Meal Programs:
    - Description: Provide access to food and meals for families in need.
    - Website: foodbankscanada.ca

Online Resources

- Government of Canada–Benefits Finder:

- - Description: A tool to help find all federal and provincial benefits you may be eligible for.
  - Website: canada.ca/en/services/benefits/finder.html
- 211 Canada:
  - Description: A helpline and online database of Canada's community and social services.
  - Website: 211.ca

These resources can provide financial assistance, support, and services to help single mothers navigate the challenges they face and improve their quality of life.

United States

Programs to consider if you are in the USA:

Federal Programs

- Temporary Assistance for Needy Families (TANF):** This program provides cash assistance to families with low incomes. The amount of assistance and the length of time it is provided varies by state.

- Supplemental Nutrition Assistance Program (SNAP): This program, also known as food stamps, provides financial assistance to help families purchase food.

- Children's Health Insurance Program (CHIP): This program provides health insurance for children in families with low incomes.

Community Resources

There are many community resources available to single parents. These resources can provide support, education, and assistance with daily tasks. Here are a few community resources to consider:

- Local food banks: Food banks can provide free or low-cost food to families in need.

- Community centers: Community centers often offer programs and services for families, such as after-school programs, sports teams, and parenting classes.

- Churches and religious organizations: Many churches and religious organizations offer support groups and assistance for single parents.

Online Resources

There are many online resources available to single parents. These resources can provide information, support, and community. Here are some online resources to consider:

- Single parent forums: Online forums can provide a community of single parents who can offer support and advice.

- Government websites: Government websites like USA.gov and Benefits.gov can provide information about government assistance programs for single parents.

Utilizing these resources can help make your journey as a single parent a little bit easier.

Chapter 25

Government Aid and Grants for Single Parents

As a single parent, it's essential to be aware of the various forms of government aid and grants available to help you navigate the financial challenges of raising a child on your own. These programs can provide crucial assistance with expenses such as housing, food, healthcare, and child care.

Types of Government Aid and Grants In The US

Here are some of the most common types of government aid and grants for single parents:

1. Temporary Assistance for Needy Families

This is a federal program that provides cash assistance to low-income families with children. The program is run by individual states and has strict work requirements. Eligible families can receive assistance for up to 60 months.

2. Supplemental Nutrition Assistance Program

This is a federal program that provides financial assistance to low-income individuals and families to purchase food. Eligible recipients receive an electronic benefits transfer (EBT) card, which can be used at participating grocery stores and retailers.

3. Women, Infants, and Children (WIC)

WIC is a federal program that provides nutrition assistance to low-income pregnant and postpartum women, as well as to their infants and young children.

The program provides healthy food, nutrition education, and breastfeeding support.

4. Housing Choice Voucher Program

This federal program provides rental assistance to low-income families, the elderly, and people with disabilities. Eligible families receive a voucher that can be used to rent private housing that meets program requirements.

5. Head Start and Early Head Start

Head Start and Early Head Start are federal programs that provide comprehensive early childhood education, health, and nutrition services to low-income children and their families. The programs are designed to promote school readiness and support healthy development.

6. Child Care and Development Fund

Another type of federal program, it provides child care assistance to low-income families. The program helps families pay for child care so the adults can work or attend training or education programs.

7. Low Income Home Energy Assistance Program

This is a federal programe that provides assistance with heating and cooling costs to low-income households. It can help with energy bills, energy crisis situations, and weatherization and energy-related home repairs.

Applying for Government Aid and Grants

To apply for government aid or a grant, you will need to contact your state or local government agency responsible for administering each program. You can find contact information and application instructions on the agency's website or by calling the agency directly.

When applying for assistance, be prepared to provide documentation such as proof of income, residency, and family size. The application process may vary depending on the program, so it's essential to follow the instructions carefully and provide all necessary information.

There are resources available to help you overcome financial obstacles. By taking advantage of government aid and grants, you can provide for you and your children.

Chapter 26

Community Programs

There are community programs and services for solo parenting superstars like you! These resources can be game-changers in helping you navigate the joys and challenges of single parenting. Let's dive right in!

Government Assistance Programs

Government assistance programs provide vital support to single parents by offering financial help and services. Some popular programs also include:

1. Section 8 Housing Choice Voucher Program: This program assists eligible families with finding safe and affordable housing in the private market.

2. Children's Health Insurance Program (CHIP): CHIP provides low-cost health coverage for children from families who earn too much to qualify for Medicaid but can't afford private insurance.

Local Community Resources

Local community resources offer a wide range of support tailored to your specific needs. Here are some examples:

1. Community centers: Community centers often provide after-school programs, recreational activities, and support groups for single parents.

2. Libraries: Libraries offer free educational resources, workshops, and activities for both parents and children.

3. Places of worship: Many religious organizations provide single-parent support groups, counseling, and financial assistance.

4. Non-profit organizations: Non-profits like United Way, Catholic Charities, and the YMCA offer

various services, such as counseling, financial assistance, and child care.

Online Support Communities

Be connected with single parents from all over the world, by online platforms sharing experiences, offering advice, and receiving emotional support. Some popular online communities include:

1. Facebook groups: Numerous Facebook groups cater specifically to single parents, offering a space to connect and share advice.

2. Reddit: Subreddits like r/single parents and r/divorce provide a wealth of information and support for single parents.

Scholarships and Educational Resources

Education is a powerful tool for personal growth and financial stability. Single parents can access various scholarships, grants, and educational resources, including:

1. Scholarships for single parents: Many organizations offer scholarships specifically for single parents.

Websites like FastWeb, Cappex, and Scholarships.com can help you find opportunities.

2. Federal Student Aid (FSA): FSA provides financial assistance for students, including single parents, to help cover the cost of higher education.

3. Online learning platforms: Platforms like Coursera, edX, and Udemy offer flexible and affordable online courses for single parents to learn new skills and advance their careers.

Remember, exploring community programs and services is an ongoing process. New resources become available all the time, so stay informed. You're doing an amazing job, and there's a whole community of people out there ready to support you!

Chapter 27

Creating a Stable and Nurturing Environment

An important goal is to create a stable and nurturing environment for your child. This means providing a safe, consistent, and loving home where your child can grow and thrive. Here are some tips to help you achieve this:

Establish a Routine

Children thrive on routine and predictability. Establishing a daily routine can help your child feel more secure and help them understand what is expected of them. This can include regular times for meals, homework, play, and bedtime.

Create a Consistent Home

Creating a consistent home environment can help your child feel more secure and grounded. This means having consistent rules and expectations for behavior, as well as creating a physical space that is comfortable and familiar. This can include having a designated space for your child to play and do homework, as well as for displaying their artwork and accomplishments.

Provide Emotional Support

Children need emotional support and validation from their parents. It is important to make time for your child and listen to their thoughts and feelings. This can help them feel heard, understood, and loved. It's also important to be patient and avoid getting frustrated or angry, as this can create a negative environment for your child.

Foster a Positive Environment

Creating a positive environment can help your child feel happy, secure, and confident. This means avoiding negative talk and criticism, and instead focusing on positive reinforcement and encouragement. You can also foster a positive environment by engaging in fun and enjoyable activities with your child, such as playing games, going for walks, or cooking together.

Take Care of Yourself

As a single parent, it's important to take care of yourself in order to provide a stable and nurturing environment for your child. This means making time for self-care. It's also important to seek support from friends and family.

Taking care of yourself is not selfish—it's essential for your own well-being and for the well-being of your child.

You can create a stable and nurturing environment for your child as a single parent. Remember, it's not always easy, but with patience, love, and dedication, you can provide a wonderful home.

Chapter 28

Establishing Routines: A Key to Successful Solo Parenting

There is one strategy that can make a significant difference in your life and the lives of your children; establishing routines.

Routines provide a sense of structure and predictability. By creating consistent daily, weekly, and even monthly routines, you can:

- Reduce stress and anxiety: When you know what to expect and when to expect it, you can better manage your time and resources.

- Improve behavior: Consistent routines help children understand what is expected of them, which can lead to better behavior and fewer tantrums.

- Foster independence: As your children become familiar with the routines, they can begin to take on more responsibility for themselves.

- Strengthen family bonds: Routines provide opportunities for quality time together, which can help strengthen family bonds and create lasting memories.

Here are some tips for establishing effective routines:

- Keep it simple: Start with simple routines that are easy to follow. You can always add more complexity as your children become more comfortable with the routines.

- Be consistent: Consistency is key when it comes to routines. Make sure to follow the routines as closely as possible every day.

- Involve your children: Children are more likely to follow routines if they feel involved in the process. Ask for their input and make sure they understand the purpose of each routine.

- Make it fun: Routines don't have to be boring. Incorporate games, songs, or other fun activities to make the routines more engaging.

- Be flexible: While consistency is important, it's also important to be flexible. There will be times when you need to adjust the routines.

Here are some examples of routines you might consider:

- Daily routines: Establish a consistent daily routine that includes time for meals, homework, play, and bedtime.

- Weekly routines: Consider establishing weekly routines such as family game night, movie night, or a special outing.

- Chore routines: Assign age-appropriate chores to your children and establish a routine for completing them.

- Mealtime routines: Establish a routine for meal planning, grocery shopping, and cooking.

Establishing routines takes time and patience. Don't be discouraged if it takes a while for your children to adjust.

With consistency and persistence, you can create routines that will make your life as a single parent easier and more fulfilling.

Chapter 29

Fostering Open Communication

Open communication is a crucial aspect of successful solo parenting. It helps to build trust, resolve conflicts, and strengthen the bond between you and your child. Here are some tips on how to foster open communication with your child:

Create a Safe Space

Make sure your child feels comfortable and safe when communicating with you. Avoid criticizing or judging them, and let them know that they can share anything with you without fear of punishment or rejection.

Listen Actively

When your child speaks, give them your full attention.

Nod, maintain eye contact, and ask questions to show that you are engaged in the conversation.

Validate Their Feelings

Acknowledge your child's feelings and emotions. Let them know that it's okay to feel the way they do, and offer comfort and support.

Use Simple and Clear Language

When communicating with your child, use language that they can understand. Avoid using complex words or phrases that may confuse them.

Encourage Honesty

Encourage your child to be honest with you, even when the truth is difficult to hear. Let them know that you will always love and support them, no matter what.

Practice Patience

Open communication takes time and practice. Be patient with your child, and don't rush them to share their thoughts and feelings.

Lead by Example

Show your child the importance of open communication by being open and honest in your own communication. Let them see that it's okay to express themselves and share their thoughts and feelings.

By fostering open communication with your child, you can create a strong and healthy relationship based on trust, respect, and understanding.

Chapter 30

Growing as a Single Parent

As a solo parent, you have the unique opportunity to grow and develop in ways that you may not have anticipated. In this section, we will explore the personal growth that can come from solo parenting and how you can embrace it to become a stronger, more resilient person.

Growth Mindset

The first step in personal growth as a solo parent is adopting a growth mindset. This means believing that you can grow and develop through challenges and setbacks. It also means embracing mistakes and learning from them, rather than seeing them as failures.

You will face many challenges and obstacles. You may struggle with feelings of isolation, overwhelm, and self-doubt. But by adopting a growth mindset, you can reframe these challenges as opportunities for growth and learning.

Self-Care

When you take care of yourself, you are better able to take care of your children and manage the demands of solo parenting.

Self-care can take many forms, including:

- Getting enough sleep
- Eating a healthy diet
- Exercising regularly
- Practicing mindfulness or meditation
- Engaging in hobbies or activities that bring you joy

It's important to prioritize self-care and make it a regular part of your routine, even when it feels like there isn't enough time in the day.

Building a Support Network

Having a support network can also provide practical help, such as child care or emotional support. Don't be afraid to reach out and ask for help when you need it.

Personal Development

Personal development is an ongoing process of learning and growth. You may find that you have more time for personal development than you did when you were in a relationship.

There are many ways to pursue personal development, including:

- Reading books or articles on topics that interest you
- Taking online courses or attending workshops
- Joining a book club or discussion group
- Hiring a coach or therapist

- Practicing gratitude or journaling

Embracing Change

Finally, personal growth as a solo parent requires embracing change. Change can be scary, but it can also be exciting and full of possibility.

You have the opportunity to create a new life for yourself and your children. Embrace this opportunity and be open to new experiences, even if they feel uncomfortable or uncertain at first.

By adopting a growth mindset, practicing self-care, building a support network, pursuing personal development, and embracing change, you can become a stronger, more resilient person. Someone may look to your wisdom and expert advice.

Chapter 31

Resource Books

Here are some recommended readings for further learning about solo parenting:

Books

The 5 Love Languages of Teenagers: The Secret to Loving Teens Effectively by Gary Chapman—While not specifically about solo parenting, this book offers valuable insights into how to communicate with and show love to teenagers. It can be helpful for single parents who are trying to navigate the challenges of raising teens on their own.

The Conscious Parent: Transforming Ourselves, Empowering Our Children by Dr. Shefali Tsabary—This book encourages parents to look inward and examine their own emotions and behaviors, rather than simply focusing on their children's actions. It can be a helpful resource for single parents who are looking to improve their parenting skills and build a stronger connection with their children.

Inspirational Quotes for Single Parents

The inspiration for this book came about when I was asked, "What was I most proud of in my life and what was I good at?"Although there are many accomplishments in my life, there are none that mean as much to me as being able to take care of my two daughters. They are my pillars of strength. I enjoy a great quote.

 Listed below are a few quotes for you to read and take pleasure. I am hoping that some of them might resonate with you and bring you peace, confidence, and joy. It's important to find inspiration and motivation to help you navigate the ups and downs of solo parenting. Enjoy the inspirational quotes. Remember to stay strong and focused on your journey always!

"The most important thing a father can do for his children is to love their mother." — Theodore Hesburgh

"The heart of a mother is a deep abyss at the bottom of which you will always find forgiveness." — Honoré de Balzac

"Single moms: You are a doctor, a teacher, a nurse, a maid, a cook, a referee, a heroine, a provider, a defender, a protector, a true superwoman. Wear your cape proudly."
—Mandy Hale

"I am prouder of my years as a single mother than of any other part of my life." — J.K. Rowling

"Being a single parent is not a life full of struggles, but a journey for the strong." — Meg Lowrey

"The strength of a single mother is greater than the natural laws." — Unknown

"Remember that a single mom is just like any other mom and that our number one priority is still our kids. Any parent does whatever it takes for their kids, and a single mother is no different." — Paula Miranda

"Just because I am a single mother doesn't mean I cannot be a success." — Yvonne Kaloki

"I didn't set out to be a single mom. I set out to be the best mom I could be . . . and that hasn't changed." — Unknown

"When you look at your mother, you are looking at the purest love you will ever know." — Mitch Albom

"Some days she has no idea how she'll do it. But every single day it still gets done." — Unknown

"Being a single parent made me stronger than ever before." — Unknown

"Being a single parent is twice the work, twice the stress, and twice the tears but also twice the hugs, twice the love, and twice the pride." — Unknown

"Being a working mother and a working single parent instills in you a sense of determination." — Felicity Jones

"The moment a child is born, the mother is also born. She never existed before. The woman existed, but the mother, never. A mother is something absolutely new." — Rajneesh

"Being raised by a single mother, I learned to appreciate and value independent women." — Kenny Conley

"My mother was a single mom, and most of the women I know are strong." — Regina King

"A single mom tries when things are hard. She never gives up. She believes in her family, even when things are tough. She knows that above all things, love is a choice, and she chooses to love even when it's hard." — Unknown

"Being a single parent is about strength, courage, and perseverance." — Unknown

"A single mother has a backbone made of steel and a heart made of gold." — Unknown

In Conclusion

As we reach the end of this journey together, I want to extend my heartfelt gratitude to every single mother and child who has walked this path with me. Remember, the challenges we face are formidable, but our love, resilience, and determination are far greater. You are the backbone of your family, the source of endless love and strength. Your tireless dedication and unwavering spirit are truly inspiring. And to the children, never forget the immense pride and joy you bring to your mother's life. Together, we are not just surviving; we are thriving, building a future filled with hope and boundless possibilities.

To the parents that are struggling and are doing their best, hang in there because the dark clouds are temporary and the rainbows will shine thru. My daughters have been my rainbows, that gave me strength. I can say that my daughters have grown up to be beautiful young woman. Every person that meets my daughters express how very proud of them they are. People congratulate me on how I have raised extraordinary woman. My daughters are successful woman, who manage their own businesses and one day will have children of their own. They will do amazing jobs raising their children. I have confidence in stating that, I have been a great inspiration and mentor to them. Keep believing in yourselves, keep supporting one another, and always remember that you are stronger than you know. Thank you for allowing me to share this guided journey with you. I hope that you find value in the tools that have been provided. Here's to the beautiful, resilient, and extraordinary journey of single parenthood.

www.ingramcontent.com/pod-product-compliance
Lightning Source LLC
Chambersburg PA
CBHW060500010526
44118CB00018B/2477